PIPPI LONGSTOCKING

by
Astrid Lindgren

Teacher Guide

Written by
Anne Troy

Note

The Puffin paperback edition of the book was used to prepare this guide. The page references may differ in other editions.

Please note: Please assess the appropriateness of this book for the age level and maturity of your students prior to reading and discussing it with your class.

ISBN 1-56137-036-3

To order, contact your local school supply store, or—

Novel Units, Inc.
P.O. Box 791610
San Antonio, TX 78279

Web site: www.educyberstor.com

Table of Contents

Skills and Strategies

Comprehension
  Predicting, comparison/
  contrast, sequencing

Listening/Speaking
  Discussion, drama,
  improvisation

Writing
  Similes

Vocabulary
  Word mapping, sorting

Thinking
  Brainstorming

Literary Elements
  Fantasy genre, story map,
  characterization

Summary of *Pippi Longstocking*

The plot of *Pippi Longstocking* is a series of episodes in the life of a silly little girl who lives without any grownups in a little house at the edge of a village. A horse and a monkey live with Pippi and she has two friends, Tommy and Annika, who spend a great deal of time with her because of the unusual fun she offers.

Introductory Activities

1. Look at the picture on the cover of the book. Can you find any clues about this story? What type of story might this be? Why do you think that? (The teacher's role is to accept student predictions, making no judgment about the correctness. The teacher follows with probing questions that will help students give reasons or evidence for their predictions.)

2. Pippi has a very active imagination. She sometimes exaggerates. What is the difference between exaggeration and a lie? Brainstorm the meanings of both words. Write each word in a circle with lines and ask the children for their first response when they hear the word lie. Then do the same for exaggeration. (See Activity Sheet, page 4.)

3. Tell the children that this story is a fantasy. Have the group define fantasy by using the T-Diagram.

	Realistic Story	Make-believe or Fantasy
Setting:	our world	not quite like the real world
Characters:	like us	unusual characters
Action:	could happen	never could happen
Problem:	could be ours	never could be ours
Example:	*Ramona Quimby* books	*Three Bears*

4. Imagine a new girl moved into a house on your block. What questions would you want her to answer? (The teacher will record the class responses on a large sheet of paper with the words PIPPI LONGSTOCKING in the center.)

5. Let's begin this book like we're going on a trip with a story map. We need the answers to some questions. (page 5)
   1. Who is the main character?
   2. Where does the story take place?
   3. Is the story make-believe or true-to-life?
   4. What is the problem in the story? Does the problem change or are there several problems? Your story map may change as you read *Pippi Longstocking*.

Activity Sheet

Teacher lists student responses to each word and then the class comes to a conclusion to the difference between the two words.

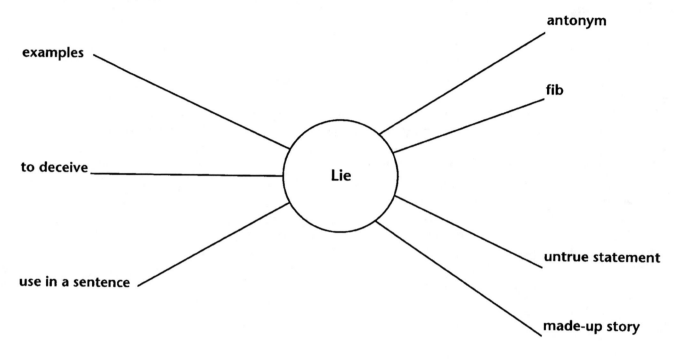

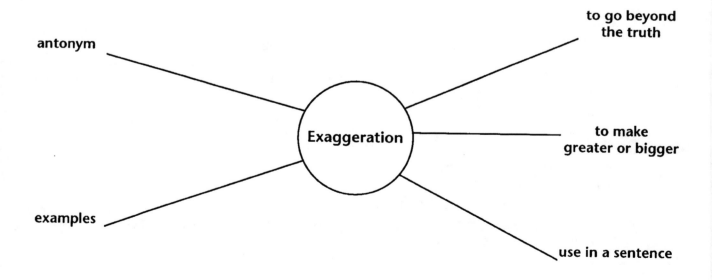

Story Map

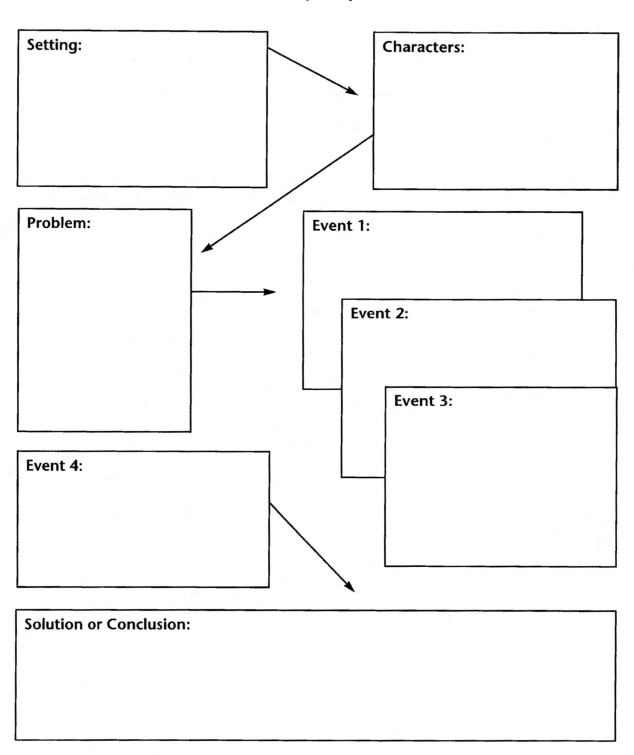

Setting:

Characters:

Problem:

Event 1:

Event 2:

Event 3:

Event 4:

Solution or Conclusion:

Using Predictions in the Novel Unit Approach

We all make predictions as we read—little guesses about what will happen next, how the conflict will be resolved, which details given by the author will be important to the plot, which details will help to fill in our sense of a character. Students should be encouraged to predict, to make sensible guesses.

As students work on predictions, these discussion questions can be used to guide them: What are some of the ways to predict? What is the process of a sophisticated reader's thinking and predicting? What clues does an author give us to help us in making our predictions? Why are some predictions more likely than others?

A prediction chart is for students to record their predictions. As each subsequent chapter is discussed, you can review and correct previous predictions. This procedure serves to focus on predictions and to review the stories.

```
┌──────────────────────────────┐
│   Use the facts and ideas the│
│        author gives.         │          ╭───────────╮
└──────────────────────────────┘         │ Use your own │
                                          │  knowledge.  │
   ╭──────────────────────────────╮       ╰───────────╯
   │ Use new information that may cause │
   │      you to change your mind.      │
   ╰──────────────────────────────╯
```

Predictions:

_____

_____

_____

_____

Prediction Chart

What characters have we met so far?	What is the conflict in the story?	What are your predictions?	Why did you make those predictions?

Using Character Webs in the Novel Unit Approach

Attribute Webs are simply a visual representation of a character from the novel. They provide a systematic way for the students to organize and recap the information they have about a particular character. Attribute webs may be used after reading the novel to recapitulate information about a particular character or completed gradually as information unfolds, done individually, or finished as a group project.

One type of character attribute web uses these divisions:

- How a character acts and feels. (How does the character act? How do you think the character feels? How would you feel if this happened to you?)

- How a character looks. (Close your eyes and picture the character. Describe him/her to me.)

- Where a character lives. (Where and when does the character live?)

- How others feel about the character. (How does another specific character feel about our character?)

In group discussion about the student attribute webs and specific characters, the teacher can ask for backup proof from the novel. You can also include inferential thinking.

Attribute webs need not be confined to characters. They may also be used to organize information about a concept, object or place.

Attribute Web

The attribute web below is designed to help you gather clues the author provides about what a character is like. Fill in the blanks with words and phrases which tell how the character acts and looks, as well as what the character says and what others say about him or her.

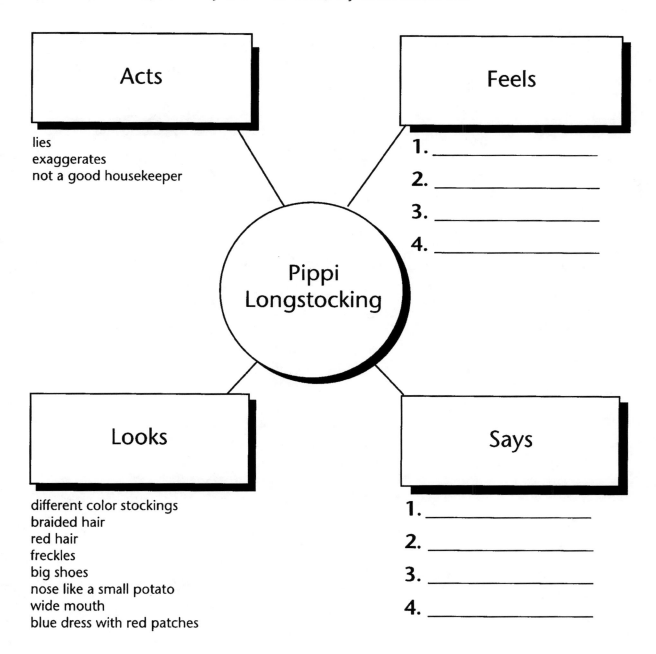

Acts

lies
exaggerates
not a good housekeeper

Feels

1. _____
2. _____
3. _____
4. _____

Pippi Longstocking

Looks

different color stockings
braided hair
red hair
freckles
big shoes
nose like a small potato
wide mouth
blue dress with red patches

Says

1. _____
2. _____
3. _____
4. _____

Attribute Web

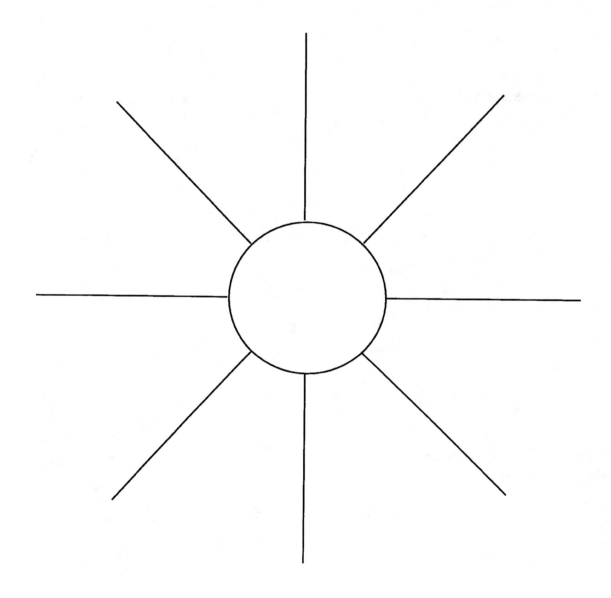

Chapter 1—Pippi Moves Into Villa Villekulla

Vocabulary

satisfaction (12)	cannibal (12)
remarkable (13)	promenade (15)

Discussion Questions and Activities

1. List all the unusual things about Pippi.
   - strange clothes
   - monkey sits on her shoulder
   - she walks with one foot in the gutter
   - she walks backwards
   - she broke heads by throwing them in the air
   - she made pancake batter with the bath brush
   - her horse lives on the porch
   - she lives all by herself
2. What is Pippi's reason for telling lies? *(p. 18, The people in the Congo tell lies all day long and Pippi stayed there too long.)*
3. Why do you think Tommy and Annika had a good time with Pippi? *(Answers will vary.)*
4. Pippi did what she wanted to do every day because she had no parents to tell her what to do. Suppose you had no parents and had to take care of yourself. What would you do? *(Answers will vary.)*
5. Pippi invited her friends for a breakfast of pancakes. Suppose you lived by yourself and you invited friends over for breakfast. What would you serve? Think of the steps you would follow and the possible difficulties you might have. *(Answers will vary.)*
6. Begin an attribute web for Pippi. (See page 9 of this guide.)

Chapter 2—Pippi Is a Thing-Finder and Gets Into a Fight

Vocabulary

bannister (24)	emphatically (37)

Discussion Questions and Activities

1. **Prediction:** Look at the chapter title. What do you think a Thing-finder is? Teacher writes class responses and after the chapter is read answers are verified.
2. What was unusual about the way Pippi baked cookies? Why wouldn't you like to eat Pippi's cookies? *(She rolled the dough on the floor.)*
3. Pippi found some unusual things. The teacher will have the class list them.
   - old man lying asleep
   - rusty tin can
   - empty spool of thread
4. Pretend you are a "Thing-finder." You are searching for "things" in a junkyard. You find something very unusual. Draw a picture of what you found. Think of different and unusual ways to use your "thing." List the uses below your picture.

5. Bengt and the other boys teased Pippi. Suppose you were teased by some boys. What would you do? List alternatives.

Pippi's Actions	Alternatives
hung Bengt in a tree	
set one boy on a gate post	
threw one boy over the fence	
put one boy in a toy cart	

Chapter 3—Pippi Plays Tag with Some Policeman
Vocabulary
fragrance (38) rhubarb (39)
haughtily (40) reproach (40)

Discussion Questions and Activities
1. **Prediction:** What do you think will happen in this chapter based on the title? Could this be dangerous for Pippi? Why? *(Answers will vary.)*
2. What would happen to you if you had no mother, father, or relatives? Why were the policemen looking for Pippi? *(p. 39, Answers will vary.)*
3. The policeman tried to convince Pippi that it was important to go to school. If you were the policeman, what would you say? Role Play.
3. What techniques did the author use to make Pippi's game of tag with the policeman funny? *(Answers will vary.)*
4. Why did the policeman decide that Pippi did not belong in a children's home? *(p. 46, Answers will vary.)*
5. If you were Tommy and Annika what would you have said to Pippi about her game of tag with the policeman? Role Play.
6. Do you think your parents would like you to have a friend like Pippi? Why or why not? *(Answers will vary.)*

Chapter 4—Pippi Goes to School
Vocabulary
somersaults (48) heedless (51) contritely (52)
hazarded (52) extravagant (54) ibex (54)
unruly (55) decently (58) astonished (58)

Discussion Questions and Activities
1. Why did Pippi decide to go to school? *(p. 50, So she would get Christmas, Easter, and summer vacation.)* Why is this funny? *(Answers will vary.)*

2. Why did the teacher have trouble with Pippi? Was it the teacher's fault or Pippi's? *(Answers will vary.)*
3. If you had a pupil like Pippi drawing on the floor, what would you do with her? *(Answers will vary.)*
4. Why doesn't Pippi know how to behave in school? *(p. 59, She doesn't have a mother, her father is a cannibal king and she's sailed on the ocean all her life.)*
5. Would you like to go to school in Argentina? Why or why not? *(p. 60, Answers will vary.)*
6. Make a chart listing reasons for going to school and for not going to school.

Reasons for going to school	Reasons for not going to school
learn to read and write	more time to play
have fun with friends	

7. If you were Pippi's teacher, how would you have made her behave? *(Answers will vary.)*

Chapter 5—Pippi Sits on the Gate and Climbs a Tree
Vocabulary

crestfallen (63)   ridiculous (64)   pension (71)
dungeon (71)   foliage (72)

Discussion Questions and Activities
1. Pippi says lots of silly things. She has not gone to school, and she has not studied geography but she talks about many faraway places where she has visited. Let's find the countries she talks about on the map. What are some of the countries?
   • p. 17—Egypt—people walking backward
   • p. 17—India—people walking on their hands
   • p. 41—Portugal
   • p. 55—India—fight with a huge snake
   • p. 60—Argentina—against the law to have lessons
   • p. 63—Shanghai, China—man with big ears that reached to his shoulders
   • p. 65—Chinese eat swallow's nest
2. Why do you think Pippi makes up all these stories? *(Answers will vary.)*
3. Pippi, Tommy and Annika have a secret hiding place in the tree. Draw a picture of a secret hiding place you have had. Write three sentences that tell why your place is special.
4. **Prediction:** Look at the next chapter title. What wild things could happen on a picnic with Pippi? (Teacher lists responses on the board.)

Chapter 6—Pippi Arranges a Picnic

Vocabulary

injustice (75)	nimbly (76)	radiant (78)	acquainted (80)
expedition (82)	exasperating (83)	tolerate (84)	

Discussion Questions and Activities

1. What do you bring in a picnic basket? *(Answers will vary.)*
2. What kind of picnic spot do you look for? What do you avoid? *(Answers will vary.)*
3. What is the worst thing that could happen on a picnic? *(Answers will vary. Teacher lists responses for each of the above.)*
4. What were the silly things Pippi said and did? *(Teacher puts the following sketch on large paper and adds points as the children respond.)*

Pippi's Picnic

Said	Did
p. 80 "I don't want to sit with the ants because I'm not acquainted ..."	p. 81 decides to fly
	p. 82 threw shoe in water
p. 80 "Bite them back."	p. 84 pulled bull's tail
p. 80 "1, 2, 19, etc."	p. 85 rode bull

5. **Prediction:** The next chapter title gives us clues to where Pippi goes, but what do you think she will do at the circus?

Chapter 7—Pippi Goes to the Circus

Vocabulary

goggling (90)	millstone (91)	suspiciously (91)	disgustedly (92)
astonishment (92)	frock (93)	mechanism (97)	taut (97)
impudent (100)	scornfully (102)		

Discussion Questions and Activities

1. Why do Pippi's actions make people angry? List all the people Pippi disturbed in this book. (Sequence Activity) Teacher may have characters listed on strips of paper and the class has to put them in order.

   Chapter 1—Bengt and boys
   Chapter 2—policemen
   Chapter 3—teacher
   Chapter 5—girl
   Chapter 6—circus people

   >Miss Carmencita
   >Miss Elvira
   >Ringmaster
   >Mighty Adolf

2. The author describes Pippi's red hair. The boys teased Pippi and compared her hair to a red hot fire. Think of many different things that Pippi's hair could be compared to.

Pippi's hair is as red as_____.

Chapter 8—Pippi Entertains Two Burglars
Vocabulary
encouragingly (106)   shottische (107)   gravely (109)   unmercifully (112)

Discussion Questions and Activities
1. **Prediction:** How do we usually entertain someone? What will Pippi do with the burglars? (List class responses.)
2. How did Pippi handle the burglars? *(p. 110, She picked them up and put them on the wardrobe, poked her finger at them and tied them up with rope.)*
3. Why did Pippi cut the ropes and free the burglars? *(p. 112, So they could dance with her.)*
4. Why do you suppose Pippi gave the burglars money? *(Answers will vary.)*
5. Mr. Nilsson did not help Pippi with the burglars. The horse was no help. These were very special pets. If you had a choice for an unusual pet, what would it be? Why would you choose this pet? How would it fit into your family? Write three sentences answering these questions and be ready to share with a classmate.
6. Would Pippi fit into your family? Would you like to adopt a sister like Pippi? Why or why not?
7. What problems would your mother have with a child like Pippi? What problems would your father have with a child like Pippi?

Chapter 9—Pippi Goes to a Coffee Party
Vocabulary
grudgingly (116)   sternly (122)   granulated (123)   apparently (124)
chilblains (124)   twiddled (125)   outrageously (126)

Discussion Questions and Activities
1. **Prediction:** If you invited a friend to a party, how would you expect her to behave? What do you think Pippi might do? (List class predictions.)
2. Why would Pippi worry about how to behave at a coffee party when she never behaves the right way? *(Answers will vary.)*
3. Pippi and the ladies complained about servants. What was Pippi's wildest exaggeration? Which was the funniest? *(Answers will vary.)*

Chapter 10—Pippi Acts as a Lifesaver
Discussion Questions and Activities

1. Pippi saved two little boys from a fire. What is the bravest thing you have ever done? Was Pippi brave or foolish? Is it sometimes hard to tell the difference between what is brave and what is foolish? Why?

Brave	Foolish
courageous	silly
bold	not wise
without fear	

Chapter 11—Pippi Celebrates Her Birthday
Vocabulary

mournfully (146)	customary (149)	dictation (151)	consoled (155)
circumstances (155)	enchanted (159)	bellow (160)	

Discussion Questions and Activities

1. **Prediction:** What do you usually expect for a birthday? What will Pippi do on her birthday? How will it be different from yours? (Teacher lists three sets of predictions.)
2. What is another way for Pippi to say, "With this I can almost see the fleas in South America"? (p. 160, Answers will vary.)
3. What kind of party would you like for your next birthday? (Answers will vary.)
   Make a plan for your party. Write sentences that tell:
   - food you might serve
   - number of guests you'd invite
   - games you would play
   - time of day and place for the party
   - problems you might have with your party
4. Which of Pippi's characteristics would you like to possess? Which characteristics would you like to avoid? Why? (Answers will vary.)

Supplementary Activities

Drama Activities

1. **Transforming:** Start in a circle and make an imaginary object in your hands. Pantomime and outline your object so others can visualize the object clearly. Then pass your object to the next person who will take your object and remold it into something else.
2. **The Machine:** One person begins an action with an accompanying noise. Each person connects himself in some manner and adds a new movement and noise. Teacher can move around and remove people so they can put themselves in a new position.
3. **Team Sports:** Divide class into two teams and choose a sport (such as volleyball). Begin an imaginary game with members pretending to bat a ball around.
4. **Tug-of-War:** Two players play tug-of-war with an imaginary rope.
5. **Playball:** Group first decides on the size of the ball, and then the members toss the ball among themselves on stage. Once the game is in motion the teacher calls out that the ball is becoming various weights.
6. **Involvement:** Group agrees on an object which cannot be used without involving all of them. They are to participate in a joint action which all move the same thing. (e.g., pulling a fishnet, pushing a stalled car, taffy pulling, etc.)

Improvisations

1. **Performing a Task:** Pick a simple task (such as picking up a stool) and perform that task a different way each time. (e.g., as an older person, as a child, as a weight lifter, etc.)
2. **Situations:** Teacher picks a "where" and class as a small group acts out that situation. (i.e., group sitting in front of a theatre for 2 hours—waiting in 102° temperature)
3. **Airport:** Each person (6) enters the room with a separate identity and purpose. During the course of the waiting period s/he must make his/her identity and purpose known through his actions.

Writing

Post a large sheet of paper on a bulletin board and encourage children to write on the paper. Here are suggestions for "directed graffiti."

Special Activities

1. Post a large crossword puzzle with words and definitions for the novel. Students can work on it and learn new vocabulary in their spare time.
2. Have an Exaggeration Contest. Ask students to write the wildest exaggeration they can think of in a designated space on the bulletin board. Only one sentence, please! Give prizes for the biggest, funniest, tiniest, strangest.

Story Sequences

When the class has finished reading a chapter or the novel, try this game for practice in sequencing events. Pick 10 major events in the book and think of a sentence that describes each event. Print the first half of each sentence on one sheet of paper, in the order in which the events take place. Print the second half of each sentence on 10 separate slips of paper. Now have students choose partners. Give each pair the sheet of paper with the sentence beginnings and ask them to match them with the 10 slips that have endings. Have children make up their own sequence-match sheets for others to try.

Summarizing Activity

Cut out each of the boxes and put them face down on a table. Let student (or small group) turn one over and give their answer.

Funniest Part	Most Interesting Part	Most Beautiful Words
Best-liked Character	The Author	Saddest Part
Favorite Picture(s)	Plot of the Story	Setting time and place
Most Exciting Part		

Clothes for Pippi Longstocking

Pippi had strange clothes. Make and decorate a T-shirt and stockings for her. You may make an unusual shirt or you may make one like you would choose to wear. Make designer stockings with words to describe Pippi.

19

Vocabulary Activities

1. Develop word maps. Use color to distinguish antonyms, synonyms, etc.

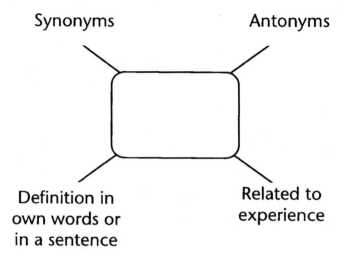

Synonyms   Antonyms

Definition in   Related to
own words or   experience
in a sentence

2. Crossword Puzzles: Have students use vocabulary words from the chapter to make crossword puzzles on graph paper. They should write a question for each word and develop an answer sheet. The teacher will check then distribute the puzzles to other students to work on in their free time.
3. One student picks a word from the vocabulary list or cards. Another student has ten (or five) questions to discover the word and give the definition.
4. List vocabulary words on a large sheet of paper. Leave room for students to a) illustrate the meaning next to each word; b) list a memory device to remember the word.
5. List the vocabulary words on the board or on a sheet of paper in the form of a table. Pronounce the words. Ask students to rate their knowledge of each word (as a group, in cooperative groups or individually).

Vocabulary Words	I Can Define	I Have Heard/Seen	I Don't Know

6. Provide vocabulary challenge words in context. Ask students to "guess" at the meaning from context, asking why for each guess. Generate a listing of the "why" answers to teach context clues.

7. Select ten words. Write only every other letter and a synonym or definition. Exchange student papers.

    Example: a_o_a *(aroma)*

8. Word Sort:

    I can say

    I know what it means

    I don't know

9. Word Sort:

    Action

    Things

    Places

    Names

10. I am thinking of a word that:

    has a long a sound

    begins with the same sound as Pat

    means _____

    is a synonym of

Pattern Writing About the Book

Directions: Finish the sentences by filling in the blanks.

Pippi Longstocking, written by _____,

is _____. The main
　　　　　(kind of book)

character is _____ who is
　　　　　　　　　　(name)

_____, _____,
　　(description)　　　　　　(description)

and _____. The story starts when
　　　(description)

_____

_____.

Next _____

_____

_____.

Then _____

_____

_____.

Finally _____

_____

_____.

Assessment for *Pippi Longstocking*

Assessment is more than a single test. The following eight items can be completed during the novel study. The student and teacher will check off the items as completed. Points may be added to indicate the level of understanding.

Name _____ Date _____

Student   Teacher

_____   _____   1.   Create a predicting chart to record ideas about the book. (See pages 6-7 of this guide.)

_____   _____   2.   Submit a finished story map. (See page 5 of this guide.)

_____   _____   3.   Draw a picture or assemble a collage for Pippi.

_____   _____   4.   What would you give to Pippi for a birthday or other celebration? Explain your choice in a short paragraph.

_____   _____   5.   Give yourself credit for each drama activity you complete.

_____   _____   6.   Complete five vocabulary activities. (See pages 20-21 of this guide.)

_____   _____   7.   Write a letter to *Pippi Longstocking*'s author, telling your reaction to the book and offering ideas for other books.

_____   _____   8.   Take a class poll on the book for use in schools. Share the results with your principal or librarian.

Comments:

Notes